"Hugs from Heaven"

"Hugs from Heaven" is an amazing and powerful journey of courage that will inspire you to be the best you can be. Linda shines out a light of hope that will uplift your spirit."
— Best selling Author "Every Word has Power" Yvonne Oswald MHT MNLP

"Linda's story reminds us all that we need to see not through our eyes, but through our hearts"
— Michelle E. DiEmanuele, President & CEO, Credit Valley Hospital

"Linda has written an inspirational and emotional story that leads to a powerful connection with the universe, and the unseen world. This is a book packed with honesty, strength and survival"
— Gina Mollicone-Long, Best-selling Author and Transformational Trainer

"This short book provides a powerful insight into the human spirit's ability to cope, survive and thrive under the most difficult of circumstances. Linda's history, from her early youth to her current state, shows how we can turn adversity to advantage no matter how bleak the situation appears to be at the time. A must read for everyone."
— John Burke, former co-worker

"An inspirational book, from a warm and open person, written to share her journey to find herself and to help others. Tragic as many of the stories are, it demonstrates a tremendous ability to learn good things from very difficult experiences. A story of healing. It is a lesson in how to do Forgiveness. This book will teach you how to get hugs from Heaven that are meant for you. When you read it, you will get your first hug from Heaven."
— Linda Stevens, retired Deputy Minister, Province of Ontario

Hugs from Heaven

(Divine Intervention)

Linda Dianne

Copyright 2009 by Linda Dianne

All rights reserved

No part of this book may be reproduced, stored in a retrieval system, or transmitted by any means, electronic, mechanical, photocopying, recording, or otherwise, without written permission from the author or publisher. There is one exception. Brief passages may be quoted in articles or reviews.

Library and Archives Canada Cataloguing in Publication

Cataloguing data available through Library and Archives Canada

ISBN 978-1-926582-30-6

Dedication

This book was written with love and appreciation
And is dedicated to my most cherished
Hug from Heaven
My wonderful loving son
Michael
Who encouraged me to write this book, and
Who has always given me his support,
His love and his friendship

This book is also for my Sister and Brothers, who
Travelled a rough road through the muddy
And cluttered childhood path that led us to
Close and seal the door of abuse that continued to
Add pain to the
Deep wounds and emotional scars
From the hidden secrets of our childhood memories

Acknowledgements

Thank you to Neil, my companion, who gave me the space and quiet time to write and for his love, support and encouragement and sitting through many readings of my words to satisfy my comfort level on the parts of my life I needed to share.

Thank you to the many friends and colleagues for their support and friendship and getting me through difficult times even when they didn't know my family secrets and the torment that haunted me.

Thank you to God, who I believe is the creator of all things, who sent the hugs to me and provided the journey and experiences written on the pages of this book.

Thank you to Jooseth, (pronounced Jo-seth) my spirit guide who helped me dry the tears of the past and see the rainbow for the future.

Thank you to my dear friend "Lynn" who believed in my abilities and pulled me out of "The Closet" and into the open to help others find their way.

Her support and encouragement to use my special gifts has led to an amazing journey.

While enjoying our cheesecake experience, her continued support and encouragement to write my story to help open the doors for others impacted my decision to write.

Thank you to Yvonne Oswald MNLP MTLT, Best Selling Author *"Every Word has Power"*
Who gave me the courage to begin my book and personally guided me
through the process with sound advice, encouragement and support.

Introduction:

After leaving a reading from a psychic that a girlfriend and I had just received, we decided to talk about the readings over a cup of tea and dessert. As she had just recently returned from New York City, we decided to celebrate by each of us ordering a piece of cheesecake to indulge ourselves as we talked about the information given to us from the psychic.

This psychic, as many before her had done, told me I was going to write a book about my life and share it to help others. I couldn't believe that my life would have anything to offer that wasn't offered already. As I relayed this information to my friend, I positioned a creamy forkful of New York Cheesecake so that I could take a bite. The cake entered my mouth with an explosion of pure joy, a bursting of delightful creamy cheese and a teasing of sweet cherries awakened my taste buds and my senses were alerted to the pure pleasure of the texture and taste and I said to my friend "this is like getting a hug from Heaven." And there, at that very moment, I decided to write a book, and the title would be "Hugs from Heaven".

I wanted to write this book for a couple of reasons; since the Universe sent me so many messages that it is something that I am supposed to do, and I also wanted to share with others the power of the universe that surrounds us and connects us all with one another.

My experiences as a child led me on a spiritual journey opening the doors of my psychic gifts to help others deal with the incredible gifts of life and death. It is not a happy journey, but it is my journey and it is rewarding, and incredible, the ups and the downs, the rejections, the abuse, the love, betrayal and the most wonderful gift ever to receive, motherhood. This book is about unconditional love, comfort and a story of forgiveness and peace. This is my life, in small doses, and filled with hugs from Heaven.

I also want to define the difference of receiving gifts from Heaven and hugs from Heaven. I have received many gifts from Heaven, we all have; they are our friends, our family, our experiences, our body, our senses, homes, jobs, talents, both spiritual and financial rewards, the gift of travel and so on.

Hugs from Heaven, are different than gifts, and we all have received them and will continue to do so. Hugs can come at a time of darkness, when loneliness spreads like an illness bedded deep within our minds, a state of unhappiness, discomfort and pain. Think of a time when you may have felt that no one would miss you, that no one cares, not even you, and you are in so much emotional pain that you can't function. This is one of the more common times that you talk to the creator of all things, and you ask the "Why" questions, and seek answers. When you are at this low point, the universe feels your vibrations slowing down, and recognizes the sadness in your cries and sends you a wave of warmth, peace and love and soon you feel comforted and loved. This is a hug from Heaven. A hug filled with the highest possible doses of love, respect, peace and comfort.

I received this hug when the doors to my life seemed to keep closing, and my very being felt unimportant to me. I craved for love, for someone to care and I called out to the universe for a hug, a feeling of love, comfort and peace. When I received the hug, it drained my emotions and cradled me into a deep sleep of peaceful bliss, and I cried from the pleasure of receiving love and found peace within my mind, body and soul. When I awoke I no longer felt lonely but felt revived with energy that consisted of gratitude, strength and courage to continue on my journey here on earth.

Hugs also come when you just ask for them. You do not have to be unhappy to receive a hug from Heaven. As we receive hugs from family, friends and colleagues you can also receive hugs from Heaven as many times as you wish. Heaven is full of hugs and the universe is always pleased to give the hugs to you. The pleasure of receiving hugs from Heaven is overwhelming, and it will be the most gratifying feeling you will ever experience.

Just ask for them, look towards Heaven and open your heart and ask. Let your mind, body and soul feel the comfort of the hug. Believe in love and happiness and send your wonderful vibrations into the universe that in return will send you a wave of vibrations that will surround your entire existence and pleasure every part of you. Love is the powerful key that unlocks the gratitude door of Heaven, and spills the crystals of love into the universe, which sprinkles the gift throughout the world.

It doesn't matter who you are, what you have done or what you believe, as long as you ask, you will always receive hugs from Heaven. Think of the Universe as your source of guidance, and understanding. Be comforted to know that the Universe is always there ready to give you exciting and wonderful gifts and hugs. Look at it this way, when you prepare to wash your clothes you separate the clothes into piles of white, delicate, colours, dark, bedding, towels etc. When you ask for a hug from Heaven you are releasing your emotional laundry into the Universe, in the care of your Guardian Angels, and like sorting laundry, the universe sorts your emotions.

Your delicate emotions are separated from the rest and are cleansed with Divine love, making them shiny and bright, and the soil from your heavy thoughts is released into the darkness and is disposed of. The colours of your emotions are cleansed and sorted so that you are only carrying your emotions, (the clothes that fit you and that are yours) and all the heaviness from the burdens of others that you carried for them are removed and bundled in a package that floats far away from you.

Your emotional laundry is gently cleansed, and neatly placed in a gift box filled with love to return to you as a gift.

Receiving your gift box will feel something like wearing clothes freshly washed that are clean and bright and have a wonderful fragrance and you will clearly see things better, and understand the power of the universe, and the hug you just received. Your emotional gift box is now ready for you to deal with, and you will find the answers you are seeking, and will have the strength to continue on your path with your hands situated firmly on the handrails of the universe that will provide for you and your Guardian Angels will keep you safe. Just ask!

18 — Linda Dianne

Chapter One
A Memory Of My First Hug From Heaven

The room was silent, and the morning sun was just beginning to rise as I sat quietly wiping the tears that flowed down my cheeks as I remembered the first hug I received from Heaven. There were probably several before this, but at 12 years of age one does not realize what Heaven really is, or the universe that connects us all together.

While my mother was at work, and my father was resting in the master bedroom upstairs after finishing the night shift with the Metropolitan Police Service, it was my turn to look after my younger sister Barbara, Barbie as we so fondly called her, our little Angel and Terrance Lee, my youngest brother who we called Terry.

Slicing a perfectly ripe and juicy watermelon for us to eat after the sandwiches I just made for lunch, the sound of a gunshot jolted us from this happy moment. I knew that my father and our neighbour Charlie had been drinking all morning and we all knew that it was safer for all of us to stay away from him when he had been drinking. But following the gun shot sound was my father's voice calling my name, Lindy, his pet name for me instead of my given name Linda.

Scared to approach the upstairs bedroom alone, for fear that he would touch me in forbidden places as he had done before, I motioned for my siblings to ascend the stairs with me. The gun went off again, and we stopped climbing the stairs and stood there listening, scared of what we might find. First there was silence, then his voice called for me again, and it sounded painful, and frightened, so I decided to enter the bedroom first, and blocked the doorway so that Barbie and Terry could not enter. When I saw that he was sitting on the bed, holding his service gun, I let down my hands that guarded the doorway, and Barbie and Terry entered the room.

The bullets that went off, while he

was trying to put the safety catch on the revolver, had penetrated the wall of the bedroom leaving identifiable holes. He was shaking, and I asked him to put the gun down. In his drunken state, he couldn't seem to be able to move his fingers to release the gun from his hand. I felt that I had no choice but to call Charlie, his drinking buddy who lived across the street to help me get my father to put down the gun. I hoped that he was not as drunk as my father and could help.

Charlie entered the bedroom, and asked my father to give him the gun. As Charlie received the gun from my father's hand, the cigarette my father had been smoking fell from his mouth onto the floor. Barbie bent down to pick it up to put it out, but at that very moment the gun went off and the bullet penetrated her skull and exited through her right eye. She was gone, my 6-year-old sister, right in front of me, and my 8-year-old brother Terry, the only sober witnesses to this tragic death. She was lying there in a pool of blood that surrounded her tiny limp body. My father gently placed her on the bed and wrapped her in a blanket. This gentle, loving, sweet little girl was dead and we were never again going to hear her sing, or watch her play, hold her hand or read her a story. We were never again going to hear her laugh or see her dance or mother her dolls. She was gone forever, our littlest angel.

I couldn't cry, I couldn't talk, I couldn't move, and yet I was not afraid. I felt like someone was there holding me, comforting me, hugging me, although visibly no one was, but I sensed it. A sense of peace surrounded me with the comfort of knowing that this was meant to be. I was 12 and yet I was older, I knew she was ok, and I knew that her time with us was a gift, a warning perhaps to value life and time with one another. This is the first time I can recall receiving a hug from Heaven. A hug so powerful that it changed my life, and put me on an unexpected spiritual journey, too young to embrace its full potential, and yet my young years knew it to be a journey of fulfillment and a path that I was destined to follow.

Chapter Two
The Right Hug At The Right Time

My second memory of a Hug from Heaven was the morning after Barbie's death. As I was a witness to the incident leading to my sister's death, and legally at age 12, you could testify in court, I was instructed to have no contact with my father, or Charlie, or my mother. Relatives quickly removed me and my siblings that evening to my Grandparent's home in Stayner, a small town near Collingwood, a place where only love existed. A place to feel safe, and loved, not at all like home, where love didn't exist, and the rooms were full of anger and abuse. My Grandmother's home was warm and loving and filled with home baking, and wonderful china, and beautiful things. And my Grandmother's arms were always ready to hug you and let you know you were special to her.

During the night, I suffered severe cramps and realized that my usually very regular period had started due to all the stress and trauma. The sight of the blood flowing from my body triggered in my mind the tiny limp body of my sister and the pool of blood that surrounded her. I couldn't sleep, and I didn't know what to do. My body was in shock but I made my way up the stairs to the bathroom. As I entered the bathroom, I was annoyed that my body had betrayed me and decided on its own to give me something else to deal with. Suddenly powerful messages came into my mind: it was my voice I heard, but not my words. The words were easy to understand but the delivery and messages were not of a young girl of twelve but that of a guiding spirit. I stood still and listened to what was being said, the voice, my voice was telling me that the blood from my body was a gift from God to remind me that life and death are natural things, and that my period was that of a blessing to let me know that my body will bring more life into the world. The cramps suddenly stopped and peacefulness surrounded me.

It was like no other feeling I had ever experienced, it was a hug from Heaven, a hug of life and knowledge and strength. I left the bathroom and then entered into my grandparent's bedroom. My grandmother was awake, and heard me as I entered the room. I was afraid to tell her that I had just left a stain on her bed sheet, but somehow she knew what had happened. Her arms opened wide, and she held me. She spoke no words, just held me and this was another hug from Heaven.

When morning came, my grandmother changed the bed sheets with no word of what had happened and never spoke of it. Being forbidden by the police to speak of the incident and because I was to testify at a Coroner's Inquest in a few weeks, I could not share with my sister and my two other brothers what had happened. Terry and I were to keep quiet about what we witnessed and as my brothers were staying at my Aunt's house, I couldn't comfort Terry who desperately needed to be. I was twelve and he was eight and now we were alone with this horrible feeling of abandonment.

Barbie and Terry were the youngest in our family, and both were special gifts to us. We had another brother Lawrence Allan (Larry) who was born with a hole in his heart and only lived for a few days. Barbie, our littlest angel was fun and cute and very loving. Her favourite story was "The Littlest Angel" and we would read the story to her night after night. She had just turned 6 on July 26th, and on August 6 left us suddenly to return home to Heaven.

Her short time on earth taught us many things about life itself, how fragile it was, and how our time here on earth can end quickly and without warning. Barbie loved playing with her dolls, and where she found the love and motherly instincts to care for her dolls certainly didn't come from our mother, they were part of Barbie and were hugs from

Heaven.

She would cart her dolls everywhere and she loved to sing. I no longer remember the sound of her sweet voice but sometimes I think I can feel her little hand in mine when I think of her. Perhaps she is guiding me and comforting me and helping me to deal with the guilt I feel of asking her and Terry to ascend the stairs with me to the master bedroom where her life on earth had ended.

Terry told me he never blamed me or even thought of blaming me for her death or his being a witness to her final moments on earth.

Terry was the only one that resembled my father in appearance and stature but he was nothing like him. Terry was sweet and artistic and had a very nice singing voice. He too was taken from us tragically in a car accident when he was in his twenties.

The last time I saw Terry was when I had visited him in the Don Jail when he was charged with breaking and entering. He was still living with our parents, and one night he came home later than he was supposed to and when he entered the house he was met with my father's fist. Terry fought back, but my father was very drunk and twice the size of Terry. He was very badly beaten and with a broken arm and swollen face and injuries to his entire body he was thrown out of the house. With no place to go, he and a couple of his friends broke into the school and slept in the library for the night. They were arrested in the morning, and charged with breaking and entering. My father completely disowned him, and Terry had to find another place to live.

Terry never received the comfort, love or guidance that he so desperately needed after witnessing Barbie's death. He was now full of anger and resentment and continued to break the law by stealing and more break and enters. He finally left Ontario and moved to British Columbia where his life was shortened when he and four others were decapitated when the vehicle they were in was pushed under a transport truck. According to the reports my brother swerved his car to avoid a vehicle that was in the wrong lane and heading towards him. By trying to escape from a head-on collision, he tried to move quickly out of the way and lost control of his car and slid under the transport truck. Everyone in the vehicle was sober and everyone died instantly.

Terry was married only a short time when he died and none of us had met his wife. His death was very hard on her and she couldn't handle the loss and tried to take her own life. Fortunately, she did not succeed.

The remains of Terry's body were shipped to Ontario so that he could be buried and the family could have closure. This sweet, loving boy tried so hard to overcome the pain in his heart and the demons that surrounded him. Terry left behind a daughter named Theresa of whom only just my Aunt and my sister have met. His daughter is a hug from Heaven from Terry and in his conversations with me he visits her each day.

When I heard of Terry's death I was saddened but knew that he finally would have the love and comfort and care that he longed for and deserved. He was indeed in a better place. As my grandmother found comfort in baking and giving to others, I found that I too needed to bake for Terry. I baked dozens of lemon cupcakes, a favourite of his, and I wouldn't stop until I almost collapsed. It was only when I finally began to cry over losing him that I stopped baking cupcakes. I brought all of them to the family reception that we had after the funeral service. When Terry communicated with me through automatic writing years later he thanked me for the cupcakes, which I had forgotten about.

My grandmother's house was always full of love and homemade baking and even now when I bake, the love and comfort of my grandparent's home flashes through my mind and I like to think of Barbie and Terry there with her in Heaven having afternoon tea and butter tarts and receiving the love they so deserve. Whenever, we pass through the town of Stayner, which is not often, I still feel my grandparent's presence and the hugs from Heaven they send to us.

Chapter Three
A Genuine Hug From A New Friend

My name and picture were plastered all over the newspapers, as the story hit the news of a Police Officer's daughter being killed with his service revolver, as his 12 year old daughter watches. My father's sister identified the body of my sister, and accompanied me to the Inquest. She was a witness to the identification of the body. The media followed us, pushing their cameras in our faces and blocking the entrance to the Courtroom. They even followed us to the washroom and shouted questions at us as they tried to snap pictures. I was so frightened that by the time it was my turn to go to the witness stand, the minute my name was called, I began to cry and then I fainted as they held up the bloody blanket that my sister was wrapped in and the clothing that my sister wore.

My Aunt held my hand tight while the decision was soon made that my testimony taken right after the incident would be all that they needed and that I did not have to talk or answer questions. Whisked away for a short recess, my aunt and I had to stay in the office of the Coroner so that the media could not have access to us. When we returned to the courtroom, I had to sit through the painful questioning of my father, and that of Charlie who had contradicted his original statement to the police.

Watching and listening to what was going on, my young twelve-year-old body shook with deliberate motion, and then suddenly went limp, and I felt my soul leave my body and look down from above. I remember feeling safe, warm and shielded from the pain that was being inflicted to the emotional wounds that had widely opened in my mind. I remember hearing soft whispers that everything will be fine, and that God chose me to witness this event because he knew that I was strong enough to handle it. I found myself back in my shaking body, with a new peace of mind from the hug from Heaven I just received. I heard the voice, the soft gentle voice and felt the comfort of being hugged and yet no one around me moved, or noticed anything.

Starting a new school after the tragic summer when my sister died was a brand new beginning for me. I was always so shy, and lived in the shadow of my older sister who protected me when neighbourhood boys would pick on me, and who tried to save me from my father's wandering hands. We were not close as sisters should be, but we cared for one another and when we were needed we were there for each other.

I was beginning high school, a different school than my sister and on my own. It was me being on my own, and not relying on her to be there in the hallway, or walking in front of me on the way home from school. It was only me this time, and I didn't know who I was. I wasn't anyone's sister at this school, and I wasn't anyone's friend, as all my neighbourhood friends were going to different schools or taking different classes than me. It was just me, all alone and terrified to speak to others, and frightened to say my name as it might invoke the memory of the summer and the death of Barbie that still festered in my heart and in my mind.

This was grade nine, a time to be me and eventually the me that was hidden among the shyness emerged and I became less shy, and completely comfortable at not being associated with the family name, or being a sister, just being me was a great feeling. It was a time when I could raise my hand in the classroom and not be afraid to answer a question, or volunteer for something. Things were going great, until one day, the cramps in my abdomen became so unbearable I had to leave the classroom and rush to the washroom. There, it happened again, my period making an unwanted appearance, and not on the scheduled date. The sight of the blood once again sent me into shock and the memory of Barbie's body lying in a pool of blood. I fainted, right there in the girls washroom, and woke up in the Nurse's office, with our family Doctor watching over me. I didn't even know who he was, and yet he had attended me on other occasions. The Doctor was called to tend to me due to my collapse and the possible relationship with my sister's death.

The school secretary, Mrs. Des Jardins was there too, and this wonderful woman held my hand open and placed a beautiful brooch in it. The brooch, which I still have today, was that of a ballerina, and her words will always be remembered. "Here is a gift for you, and each time you wear it or look at it, you will always know you have a friend". This was another hug from Heaven. God sent me a friend at a time when I so desperately needed one. He sent this friend in the form of a mother, not my mother, but someone else's mother, who was mine for a few precious moments. A mother who cared and reached out to me, and who just wanted to love and protect me.

I was sent home from school in a taxi and they had contacted my mother to get her permission. When I arrived home, she met me at the door, and said nothing at first and then told me to put the kettle on, have some tea, and then go to bed. She didn't ask me what happened, I guess she was already told, and she didn't try to comfort me. The next day, I went to school as if nothing had happened, and when I suffered this discomfort of the sight of blood again, I kept it to my self, and although near fainting was able to deal with it until the memory of blood around my sister's little body had disappeared in my mind, only to surface later when my own child fell and cut his lip and bled non stop until the ice pack on his lip eased the flow.

Receiving the gift of a brooch was the beginning of my brooch collection. I have learned to reach out to others and "pay it forward" by giving a brooch, the gift of everlasting friendship and love, to family, friends and colleagues.

My mother never talked to Terry or

me about my sister's death, it was like she didn't want to know. In fact no one talked about it and we just continued on as if nothing had happened. It never occurred to me that she was grieving the loss of a child, and perhaps blaming the death on my father's drinking. She was our mother, and we needed to have her love and support and we needed to feel safe. Perhaps she didn't know how to reach out because she too was very young and had to play the part of an adult when she was still a child.

My father left the police force, they gave him a year to decide if he wanted to return, but he couldn't face carrying a gun, the very weapon that took Barbie's life, so he resigned.

Chapter Four
A Hug Of Forgiveness

It was September and the tragic summer experience was now over, the death of my sister, the Inquest, the whispers and stares of others as recognition of my family name unveiled. It was a new beginning, and for me the start of me being me, not living in the shadow of my older sister and being just one of the family of now 5 children. This was a time for me with no barriers, no restrictions and no expectations. A time to shine, to grow and to forgive my father's addiction to alcohol that led to Barbie's death and the incest he practiced. It was time to forgive my mother whose inner strength was self-serving and her lack of tenderness and support and the ability to hug her children and let them know they were loved.

Her coldness sometimes was like a

bitterness that came from deep within her, and her childlike way of handling things left scars yet to be healed. Her ability to blame her children for things before finding out the truth was constant, as she punished us with harsh words, and hit us with whatever was closest to her, shoes, sticks, skipping ropes, brooms, wooden spoons. My mother could out swear a sailor, and her temper flared up easily. She would throw things during her temper tantrums, slam doors, scream and hit and push you until you were battered enough to ease her mind that you had been punished and then end with the threat of wait until your father hears about this.

My father and I now had a bond. We never spoke of the incident, none of us did, and he never attempted to touch me inappropriately again, and he never hit me. He became my go-to parent, the only one who actually cared about my opinion, and told me he was proud of me, and told me he loved me. And, although hesitation of getting close to his body for fear of the forbidden touching happening, he even gave father-daughter hugs. He listened to me and he heard me, and we had an unbelievable hidden communication that lasted until his death. I did not condone his actions towards my siblings or my mother and I had no respect for him or my mother. He beat them, he didn't always have to be drunk when he did, but when the blow came from my father it broke bones, dislocated limbs and bruised their body so badly that you thought they would never heal.

And yet, he never hit me, not ever, not before Barbie's death, except when my mother insisted that his belt be used with a full swing that hit my body with a powerful blow, for something that she insisted was the best punishment, and that only happened once. My mother, was a different story, she hit me so hard with a skipping rope one time on my bare legs that it left welts at the back of my knees that bled and made it difficult to sit and walk. This beating was because I didn't come in at the first call for supper, and after the beating was done, I was sent to my room with no supper.

Our family was so dysfunctional; I had a father who cared about me, and a mother who didn't want me, and told me so, in fact she didn't want any of us, pregnant at age 16, married and a mother at 17 and bingo pregnant again with me at age 18. Who could blame her, she was still a child herself, and yet it was me that she forgot to love and it was me she silently disowned when talking about her children. And yet my siblings all had a mother, beatings and all from her, but she cared about them, and yet neither of them had a father who cared. He abused them, beat them, belittled them, and my sister suffered so often from his incest addiction, his threats and his brutal blows across the face. Our home was only a house, a place to stay until you were of legal age to get out, and we all did as fast as we could.

How could a mother be so nice to strangers and treat her children with abuse and yet spend hours in the kitchen baking and decorating cookies for each person in our individual classrooms so that we could take them to school. Perhaps decorating cookies was a form of relief as it is for me today. It is a creative power like no other, and the cookies have no say in what colour of icing they would wear, or what design. Each cookie is beautiful, a work of art, a creation from the heart. Maybe she felt in control then, and later on when we had all left home, she took cake decorating lessons and won awards for her cakes. Was this her way of showing love, the occasional bake-a-thon and sharing of the master pieces she created, or was it the only time she felt in control of her life? It is sad to think of all that she missed as she lived with abuse, anger and fear. Didn't she know how to feel love, give it and receive it? Abuse is wrong, no matter where it comes from and in what form, it shouldn't exist, and yet it does.

It wasn't until I was married and had my son that my mother and I seem to switch roles. She was now the child and I the parent. For the most part, when we did things together like taking my son, her grandson, to the Canadian National Exhibition, or to the Ontario Place amusement park, or for a visit to Centre Island it was simply because I knew the way and was familiar with each of the places. I was her way of getting there. This is not to say that we didn't enjoy the outings, but not as mother and daughter but as two women and one child sharing the day together. It wasn't until these outings that I saw a different side of her, a far more pleasant side like a child enjoying childlike fun. Being married at age 17 didn't give her much time to enjoy amusement parks, and giving birth to 7 children, (only 6 survived) and married to an alcoholic and abusive husband certainly gave way to her sadness and bitterness.

She really didn't enjoy her grandson, didn't approve of his name, and hated that he was left- handed and that I wouldn't make him do things with his right hand. Often she would yell at him and order him to eat with his right hand and to colour with his right hand. I would answer back that he was left handed and going to stay that way. I loved my son for who he was, and found nothing wrong with being left handed or right handed. He was a gift, and is gifted. To this day, my son remembers her screaming at him, yes even in public, for using his left hand to eat with, and not his right hand.

I saw a vulnerable side to her, and I marvelled at her inner strength to survive, but I also resented the fact that her strength was self-serving. She blamed my sister and I for my father's violations on us, and her solution was for us to cover up our bodies at all times, and for sleeping we were to wear pyjamas and not nightgowns. Didn't she know that the bottoms slip off easily and this was not a preventive measure? She didn't stop him from beating my brothers, my sister or beating her and she wasn't able to stop him from locking us out of our home on a winter day. Yelling doesn't stop the torment or the abuse and it doesn't make things better, but she yelled anyway, at him, at us and at the universe.

My sister and I convinced my mother to let us have the day off school to talk to our Minister about my father and what was going on in our household. We spoke to the Minister, and confessed all to him and in the end his solution was now that we have told someone outside of the home this would probably be all that was needed. Just knowing that someone else knew would be enough embarrassment for our father that he would change. Who was he kidding? My sister and I knew that nothing would change, and the only ones embarrassed were the two of us.

Nothing did change, including our mother, who did nothing to stop the fear that festered in our hearts and minds. She would rather blame her children than face the fact that she was married to him and that she too abused us. She had plenty of opportunities to leave him, but with 6 children, and no job where could she go? At the time, we kids came up with all kinds of solutions, not realistic ones, but nevertheless we tried. So here we were, living in a home that had no room for love. It was too full of anger and abuse.

My siblings and I used to think that our parents had us children so that we could keep the house clean because there was no way my mother was going to. We had all the chores to do, including cooking and resented each moment of it. At age 11 or 12 my sister and I were responsible for the laundry with the use of a wringer washer, and hanging the clothes (even in the winter) on a very long clothesline, and on our hands and knees waxing and polishing hardwood floors (every Saturday), and doing some of the cooking. My brothers would help us with the dishes, and they would shovel the driveway and take out the garbage, and sometimes cut the grass. Like other children in our neighbourhood we were all responsible for keeping our rooms clean. Where was our mother, well if she wasn't visiting a neighbour, she was watching television, reading a Harlequin romance book or having a coffee on the front steps of our home.

The only time we saw our mother clean the house, and I mean really clean the house was when she was extremely angry with my father. She would polish, scrub, shine and sweep. And we knew there was going to be an explosion of words and a flaring of the temper once our father came home. We just didn't know which one of us caused it, or if he was in trouble all on his own. My mother was known to leave our father wherever he landed from a drunken fall. Sometimes, he would just make it home, and pass out in the car, on the kitchen floor, and even in the bathtub.

There is one time I can remember when she was so mad at him, we were all sent to our rooms upstairs and when he came through the door, she hit him with the broom and knocked him out. She left him right where he fell on the kitchen floor. Hiding in our rooms, scared to speak or go downstairs, we waited for a long time, wondering if she killed him and worried about our own lives. The next morning, we went downstairs as a group to the kitchen to see if he was breathing, only to find that he was not there. Sometime in the night he woke up and made his way to the sofa and fell asleep. What a relief, although many times we prayed that he would die, so that things would be better, we never really wanted it to happen. We just wanted to have a happy loving home, and for him to stop drinking.

This same women who hit her husband with a broom and hit her kids with anything that happen to be close by, would make sure that we all enjoyed Christmas. She would invent games for us to play, buy little gifts to put at each table setting, and sing. She would sing and sing. When it wasn't Christmas, she would sing country and western songs, and she had a nice singing voice, but the songs she sang were sad ones. Music was on all the time in our home, and music was a hug from heaven. My sister and I would play records on our little player, her Ricky Nelson records, and my Johnny Tilotson ones blasted through the house (when no one was home), and we sang as loud as we could and danced and danced. Music, was indeed an escape for us, and is to this day.

It has taken years for me to forgive my mother, and years of trying to understand her. My mother died suddenly at the age of 57 in front of her co-workers in the staff room where she worked. She was healthy and yet she died.

There was an Inquest into her death, and her co-workers were surprised to learn that my mother had two daughters. They all knew of my sister, but not a mention of me. The hurt still lingers but it no longer affects my life. Knowing my mother's feelings towards me, or lack of them, it really is no surprise that she didn't speak of me. It doesn't matter anymore, although I didn't know it at the time, she taught me so much.

If it wasn't for my mother's strength and fearlessness I would not have learned to be strong and fight for the things that I believe in. If my mother hadn't taken the time to bake cookies and let us help her decorate them I would not have found the joy in doing so these many years. If she hadn't taken the time to make every Christmas special I would not have found any happiness in celebrating the holidays in the house we lived in. If she didn't sing, I would not have known this wonderful way of releasing emotions, both happy and sad ones. And if she had been a more loving person and mother, I would not have learned the true value of love and at an early age how to tap into the universe for guidance, knowledge and love. Cookies, music and strength are hugs from Heaven from my mother, and I truly thank her.

Chapter Five
A Very Special Hug From Heaven

Years later, at age 21 I married a man who adored me and respected me and at age 23, I was delighted to find out that I was pregnant. I was scared to become a mother, as I had no idea of how to be one. All I knew is that my mothering would not resemble the role model I grew up with. I prayed long and hard that I would have a son. I was too frightened to have a daughter, and too ashamed to acknowledge the reasons why out loud. I didn't want a daughter because I would loose my trust in my husband, and my father, and every male that entered her life. How could I trust someone of the opposite sex with my little girl that they wouldn't harm her, and touch her as my sister and I had been touched? And when she turned age 6, how could I let her out of my sight, for fear that her little life would be taken away from me, and I would once again have to find the strength to bear witness to a death of a little girl with whom I was left in charge. My sister died, when she was in my care, and I couldn't let it happen to another child.

    God heard me loud and clear, and blessed me with the most precious gift of a son that helped me to grow and enjoy life. A life that I was denied as a child, he gave to me and shared his time with me. This wonderful gift was also the biggest hug from Heaven I ever received. A hug that still lingers, when I see him smile, and we share wonderful memories and new experiences together.

    This incredible human being is wise beyond his time here on earth, and is one of the most sensitive, caring people I have ever met. This hug from Heaven, cannot be measured, but only accepted with the pure delight and love that it brings to my very existence. His name is Michael, and as much as I would like to say that I named him after the Archangel Michael, I cannot make such a claim. I can tell you though, that as a very young girl, I heard the name Michael and loved it immediately and knew that if I had a son when I grew up, I would call him Michael, and I did.

I was very shy as a child and lived in my sister's shadow and was very comfortable there. She was very outgoing so I didn't have to do anything as she would be the centre of the circle and I could be just part of the circle. My sister always had boys chasing her and wanting to kiss her, and as for me no one told me I was pretty or desired so I believed that I wasn't. I accepted the fact that nobody will be asking for my hand in marriage, or for that matter be interested in dating me. Since I wasn't special enough for the family to celebrate my birthday, on the actual day, and make the celebration about me, how could I believe that someone would love me when my own mother didn't?

I became very suspicious of anyone

who paid me a compliment, as I truly believed that they were not telling the truth and that they would harm me. It was difficult for me to believe at anytime that I would be desired or loved so I didn't try to compete with my sister or my girlfriends for attention. I accepted the fact that I would probably have a great career as a teacher, live alone and have lots of beautiful clothes and that I would travel. The only members of the opposite sex that I seemed to attract were drunks, old men, nerds, has-beens and boys or men that like to live on the edge, an uncomfortable and foreign way of life for me. I did date during high school and was in a relationship for over 3 years but called it off once I started working and he continued his education. My dating slowed down for a while until one day I met a lifeguard in the building I was living in.

My roommates and I were at the pool and the lifeguard was flirting with me. He was a James Dean look-a-like with a little Martin Sheen added and his beautiful blue eyes were focused on me. I couldn't believe that someone this handsome and intelligent was interested in me. Two years later after he finished college we were married. He was the only man that treated me with respect, and he truly loved me. Our first few years of marriage were blissful and loving, but as we grew older our paths were changing and we couldn't walk together on different paths. Our marriage ended several years before our divorce. We are still friends, and we both are happier now with our new partners. Being loved and respected was a hug from Heaven, and having someone to share part of my journey here on earth with was also a hug from Heaven.

Chapter Six
A Loving Hug That Still Lingers

Before I had my own apartment I shared one with two roommates and we had a very special neighbour who later became my mother-in-law. I met her long before I met her son, the lifeguard in our building. This lovely lady and her husband would always stop and talk to us and keep an eye on our apartment for us. We became good neighbours, then friends long before I found out that their son was the lifeguard in our building. I had never seen them together as a family and had no idea that he lived on the same floor as us. You can imagine my surprise when I was invited to dinner at my neighbour's home and was introduced to their son. It certainly led to a very interesting evening.

When I was growing up I shared a birthday cake with my older sister, as our birthdays are only one year and two weeks apart. We always celebrated on my sister's birthday in November and her name was always first on the cake and then mine. I don't know if she ever resented sharing a birthday cake, we never discussed it, but it disturbed me tremendously. Sharing the celebration of my special day on someone else's birthday and sharing their birthday cake, not having one of my own really bothered me. Wasn't I special too?

For my13th birthday, which was only a few months after Barbie's death, I begged my parents to have my own birthday celebration and cake. I guess because it was something to be happy about since the tragic summer we had gone through, my parent's agreed to me inviting a few girlfriends over to celebrate my birthday. This was the very first time that I had my own birthday cake and the celebration was for me.

My next very own birthday cake was

when I turned 21 and my wonderful soon to be mother-in-law surprised me with a birthday cake to celebrate this special day. The cake was the most beautiful one I had ever seen. It was a doll, dressed like a model in a beautiful pink evening gown, my favourite colour (all icing) and she was standing in the middle of a flower garden made out of icing on a mirrored platform and placed as a centrepiece on the dining table. She also made a very special birthday dinner for me and celebrated my birthday. My very own celebration and very special birthday cake what a wonderful hug from Heaven!

My mother-in-law loved me unconditionally. As she was my friend first I was able to talk to her about anything and I did. When my marriage to her son was taking a wrong turn it was her that I confided in. It was this special lady that still was my loving friend even after the divorce and even when Neil and I moved in together. She sent us a beautiful Christmas centrepiece for our first Christmas together. My mother-in-law always made time for me, either lunch or dinner each year and a few phone calls in between.

Later on she found out that she had cancer and asked me to visit her. She knew she was dying and wasn't afraid and insisted that we have tea together made in a little teapot that I once gave her. As we sat in her bedroom, sipping tea, she thanked me for being a wonderful daughter-in-law, and for persuading her to join a book club with me to help her through the pain of the loss of her own mother. This was a difficult visit, and yet a remarkable one. We talked about so many things that we had experienced together and we said goodbye with so much love and fondness for one another. That was the last time I saw her and she made me promise not to cry at her funeral or that she was leaving her life here on earth. I kept that promise but years later the tears fell hard and I wept for my friend, my neighbour, my substitute mother, my mother-in-law. Having her in my life was a wonderful gift, and her love and friendship are everlasting hugs from Heaven.

Chapter Seven
A Treasured Hug

My mother had two sisters and neither of them were anything like her. We spent our summers at Wasaga Beach staying with my cousins where my Aunt made us beautiful clothes as if she had a magic sewing machine. She even made clothes for our dolls to match ours and later on she made both my sister's and my wedding gowns and our bridesmaid gowns.

I really didn't get to know my other aunt until after I was married and she lived a few miles from me. She was widowed at an early age and raised her son on her own. It was this aunt that I became very close to. We would do so many things together and sometimes it seemed that she was my mother. We talked about everything, and even got our ears pierced together. My aunt had her own ideas and opinions. Believe me you could not change her mind on anything, but despite her opinions which she freely gave, she was very kind and loving to me. She was a tremendous cook, and I learned a great deal from her. She adored my husband and loved our son and treated us all as if we were hers.

Eventually she moved to Vancouver, British Columbia and I only got to see her once a year when I flew out to spend a week with her. Just the two of us, we would have "jammy" parties, I would give her a perm and she would make my favourite meals. We would sit up all night gossiping, and switching Television channels and drinking tea. And I would practice tealeaf reading on her. She humoured me, and listened to everything I said with a grain of salt. My aunt was wonderful to me and it was so hard to believe that she and my mother were sisters. My aunt would hug me when I arrived and kiss and hug me when I left. She would make me call her the moment I got home, and she never forgot me on my birthday. No matter where she was she would call me, and she always sent me a surprise.

Her mothering skills were not the most ideal, but as an Aunt, she was perfect. She led me on a path of culture, entertainment and class. She made sure I was appropriately dressed and had the best of manners and etiquette to greet her very wealthy guests. When she would proudly introduce me to her friends, neighbours and socialites I felt so blessed to have someone openly display this fondness for me. She was proud of me, and this was a genuine hug from her, not often given but sincere when it was. This was a hug from Heaven that still lingers and is treasured.

It was the way my aunt treated me that I passed this special way of love onto my niece. I, like my aunt had done with me, took my little niece shopping and for afternoon tea in the beautiful Arcadian Court. They served tiny sandwiches and colourful jello for dessert to the little girls who attended the tea. For the ladies the traditional afternoon tea was served and I loved every moment of this special time and wonderful tradition.

I also would take my little nephew to the Canadian National Exhibition, a place he really loved. On occasion I would treat him to a lobster dinner, and watch him with pure delight as he lit up with excitement while he enjoyed his favourite meal. My aunt's love was a wonderful hug from Heaven and I miss her so much.

Chapter Eight
A Hug Unconditional And Wonderful

Love did not exist in the place we called home, but it was in abundance for all of us in my grandparent's home. How could my mother be so cold, and inflict emotional harm, and physical harm on her children, when her mother, our grandmother gave us so much love. What could have happened that made her so cold, and nasty and unforgiving?

When we buried our parents years later, we all agreed without hesitation that the headstone would read "In memory of our parents", we made sure that the word "loving" was left out, as we found it difficult to use the word love and associate it with them. They were not loving and caring parents. They were bullies that abused and threatened their children, and yet I had such a different relationship with them.

My father was a father to me, but I grew up with a detachment from my mother, that was so strong it made me question my ability to become a mother, as I would never ever be anything like her, and yet I had no other role model. When she suddenly died, it was her I missed the most, and I think it was because, I was still hoping that she would say she loved me and was proud of me, and I desperately longed for a hug, a hug from my mother, but it never came. She left me here on earth without so much as a hug, a smile, or loving gesture.

I have forgiven her, it did take time, but I haven't healed even yet from the lack of love this woman had for me. This perhaps was the gift she gave to me, as my bond with my own child is so incredible, and loving and wonderful. And there is no doubt that love exists between us and with us and that it is sincere, and forever. My ability to be the mother I never had is another hug from Heaven.

I was like June Cleaver, from the Television show "Leave it to Beaver", and I was Donna Reed, and Doris Day all rolled into one. I was determined that I would not swear, and never be anything like my mother. I was so caught up into being perfect, the perfect wife, the perfect mother, the perfect neighbour, the perfect friend, and the perfect daughter- in-law that I lost my identity completely. Other than a combination of the TV moms that were the role models I used to form my mothering techniques, I had no idea who I was, and what I needed or wanted. I fought so hard not to be my mother, I forgot to be me and my soul was suffocating. The real me, was more like Bette Davis, who I admired and Mae West whose sense of humour fit mine. I absolutely enjoyed the bump and grind music, and my passion for shiny and sparkling things was the true me. And shoes, my addiction to shoes began when I was in the fourth grade.

Mrs. Thomas my grade four teacher wore red shoes. I had never seen red shoes before as we only had a pair of black shoes for winter and white shoes for the summer, and white canvas shoes for the weekends. Later we had saddle shoes, but never any coloured ones. My teacher's red shoes were all that I could concentrate on during class, as she wandered about the room. I wanted a pair of red shoes, and now have several pairs of shoes in different styles and colours. To say that shoes are a hug from Heaven would be wrong, but knowing that the only pair of shoes I have to fill are mine is a hug from Heaven.

It has only been recently that I began to swear, not proud of it, but it seems to come quite easily and sometimes it just feels good to belt out the "F" word now and again. By no means do I use the tone my mother did when swear words slipped from her mouth into the air. My swearing is quite contained and sometimes very unexpected and funny. But nevertheless it is still swearing and I will try to stop it completely some day, but right now I am using swearing as a release of frustration. It doesn't really work, but it is better than alcohol, excessive eating, smoking or drugs and certainly better than abuse.

As the real me developed and surfaced it was difficult to continue in the roles of June, Doris and Donna, so I slipped into my Bette Davis and Mae West personas and enjoyed being me for a change. Difficult at first to shed the comfort of the "homemaker" image, I enrolled in adult art classes and loved the challenge it provided. I received an Honours certificate and felt that I actually accomplished something for me by me. What a wonderful feeling, and what a wonderful hug from Heaven.

Now focusing on the real me, I needed to make some changes in my life and end a 19-year marriage that already ended behind closed doors but now how to end for good. We were young when we married, and we married for the wrong reasons and now there seemed to be no reason to stay married. Michael was seventeen, and already was feeling the strains of a stressful marriage and there was no way I was going to stay in an unhappy home. I spent my childhood in one and was never going to live that way again. So I announced that I wanted a divorce, and as soon as I could find a place I could afford

I moved out. My husband and I divided our assets together and he even helped me settle into my new apartment. Michael stayed living with his father in the house, a decision we all agreed was for the best as he was still in school and I only had a one-bedroom apartment.

After paying the first and last months' rent and moving expenses I was left with only $7 to start my new life. My friend Neil, who is now my companion, was a source of strength for me during this time as I struggled with my new existence. We had been friends since I was 19 and being 19 years older than me I trusted his judgement. Soon our friendship changed into more and we moved in together. A new beginning with a new partner was another hug from Heaven.

Our life together was difficult at first because of the age difference and the silent questions and concerns that I was substituting Neil for the loss of my father. But, we have been living together for more than 20 years and like all relationships we have had family obstacles to overcome and because of our age difference there are other obstacles that we are dealing with. Having someone to share your life with is a hug from Heaven.

Chapter Nine
Incredible And Unexpected Hugs

My grandmother was given the gift of psychic awareness and often gave tealeaf readings, astrology readings and card readings. And, my grandmother served afternoon tea, in beautiful china cups, pouring tea from a silver tea service, and with an offering of freshly baked butter tarts. This wonderful English tradition is still a favourite of mine and my sister and brothers. A comfort we all enjoy, and often practice. This tradition is love, a hug from Heaven to each of us from our grandmother. To us, there is no other way to say I love you without using words. It is a healing we understand and long for.

The gift of psychic awareness was passed on to one of my brothers and me and to my son. Our gifts are different, and yet our inner strength is so much the same. We can and do connect easily to the Universe, me through the art of tealeaf reading, cards and through the use of crystals, clairvoyance and automatic writing. My brother uses cards and clairvoyance and my son with the gift of automatic writing. These gifts are hugs from Heaven.

Each of us believes in the after life, and we believe in the communication between this life on earth and the one we cannot see. We believe in Angels, Guardian Angels, Archangels and yes we believe in ghosts (entities) and each of us truly have ghost stories from real encounters.

The psychic connection for me has helped me heal, and understand on such a level that is impossible to explain. It is like knowing things and accepting them as if you already expected them to happen. This universal connection strengthens the soul and enables you to let things be, and to accept the unexpected. It is a type of healing that is complete and yet complex as it is a gift of knowledge far beyond the realm of living on earth.

Through my readings in helping others find their purpose, their journey and guiding them on their path, heals the life of my soul deep within me, and expands my comfort zone of the use of the universe for reassurance and knowledge. Clairvoyance is a remarkable gift of overwhelming pleasure when you connect with the other side. It is a gift of acceptance and guidance, a gift to use to help others and one that I cherish.

I have always been spiritual and always believed that we all could talk to our creator without the middle person such as a Minister, or Priest. After all if we were created equal then we also had a "hot line" to God, to the Angels and to the entire universe. I practiced communication with the Universe. I didn't believe that you needed to kneel or be in a church to communicate so I communicated whenever and wherever I was. I sometimes talked out loud, but most of the time I thought my questions and waited for answers and they always came.

Some of the most powerful communications from the other side happened to me a few years ago. The first one was when Neil and I were driving home through Algonquin Park. It was an extremely bitter and cold night and the roads were slippery, and dark. There was a very heavy snowfall making it difficult to see and our radio reception had cut out. With no place to turn around we had to continue driving and while Neil drove I talked with silent prayers to the universe, to God, and to the angels.

The most incredible thing happened. For a short time the snow stopped and the road became visible and the radio that had been shut off suddenly began to play the song that my father named me after. The song was called "Linda" and I had never heard the song on the radio before, but did have an old vinyl record (78 LP) at home and heard it many times. This to me was a sign from my father on the other side keeping us safe and guiding us. This was a hug from Heaven from my father.

Another incident took place when I was writing some speaking notes for a seminar that I was coordinating. My thoughts drifted to my mother and wondered if she knew how much I wanted her to say she was proud of me and that she loved me. Suddenly, my hand started to move and the pencil I was holding began to make swirls on the paper in front of me. I lost control of my hand and watched it move without effort and write my mother's name on the paper in her handwriting and then the words "Linda I love you" were written. The tears that filled my eyes blocked me from seeing the next few words that were written.

The words written next were "I am your mother and I am proud of you". The pencil fell from my hand as I recognized my mother's handwriting and my heart started to beat so fast that I couldn't breathe. My mother communicated with me, and said she loved me, words I longed to hear from her for so many years. This was a hug from Heaven from my mother and I cherish it.

One day while I was at home listening to the radio, the song "Puff the Magic Dragon" was playing and I thought of my brother Terry who loved this song and sang it often. I decided that if my mother could communicate with me through automatic writing than I should be able to communicate with Terry by writing to him. I sat down and wrote the words "Terry", it is me Linda your sister and I would like to communicate with you".

I waited for quite some time and then my pencil began to move across the paper drawing the figure eight over and over again. Just when I was about to give up, words were being formed on the page in front of me. "Hello it is your brother Terry". Now I wasn't just going to accept that it was Terry without proof so I asked him to prove he was my brother. He wrote my name in full, and then his name and then Barbie's name, the name of our parents and then he wrote "Puff the

Magic Dragon", and drew a picture of Woody the Woodpecker which is something that I taught him to do. All I could do was smile, and with tears running down my cheeks, I told him I loved him and asked if he was ok. Our conversation continued for a while and now we communicate telepathically and it is wonderful. This was a hug from Heaven from my brother.

Another time just recently Neil and I were in Michigan driving to Mount Pleasant to a Resort that we were spending the Christmas vacation at. We were later than expected due to construction and poor weather conditions. After driving for a few hours I needed to use a washroom so we began looking for a place to stop. There seemed to be nothing around us that would accommodate the use of a washroom so we continued to drive further.

Suddenly we saw a "Big K" sign indicating that there was a plaza and a Kmart department store where we could use the facilities. We made the turn into the plaza but noticed that there were only a few vehicles in the parking lot and that the plaza seemed to be boarded up except for the Kmart Store. We went into the store, and used the facilities and on our way out bought some toothpaste at the only checkout counter open. We were only in the store for a very short time, but it looked abandoned as we noticed only one person in the store but thought that the staff must be in the back rooms.

We then continued to Mount Pleasant which was about a 30 minute drive from where we had stopped. On the day we were leaving the Resort to return to Canada, we asked directions to the Kmart store so that we could stop there. To our surprise we were told that there had not been a Kmart store in that area of Michigan for several years.

We described approximately where we pulled off the highway to go to the plaza, and they searched on the computer for the plaza and the location of the Kmart store. There was nothing listed and so we followed our same route on the way home and could not find the plaza or the "Big K" sign, or Kmart anywhere. We have vacationed in the same Resort a few times since then and each time searched for the Kmart Department store. My mother worked for Kmart, and had died in a Kmart store. Could this have been my mother and the angels working together to find us a washroom? That would explain the lack of vehicles in the parking lot and the boarded up stores of the plaza. Was this a hug from Heaven? This mysterious store that seems to have disappeared but miraculously appeared when we needed to stop is beyond chance and we are holding onto the thought and believe that it was a hug from Heaven.

The universe is a source of knowledge and healing for me, and a constant guide for my journey here on earth. I have tapped into the knowledge and love that is constant and I use my gift to help others. For years I tried to ignore the messages I was receiving from the universe as I wasn't sure what to do with them and

I was frightened to tell people what I knew. As I got older and began to have visions and suddenly I would know something that I couldn't possibly have known without someone telling me, then I asked for guidance.

At first the visions were very graphic and came at me so fast that sometimes I couldn't understand what was being shown. I have a friend that is psychic and I turned to her for help. She guided me on accepting and using my gift to help others, and helped me to have control of what I saw. I promised God that I would help all those that come to me for help with my psychic gifts but I would not advertise for clients. This way if they found me I would know that I could help them and that God had sent them to me.

Through the years I have had many people come to me for help and the universe has always provided me with the knowledge and wisdom to use the knowledge in helping others. My abilities still surprise me even though I know that the universe and the angels guide me and protect me. It is a wonderful feeling when you can take away a burden that has been bothering someone and letting each know that they are loved and not alone.

I had the wonderful opportunity of attending a session with Doreen Virtue a world-renowned psychic healer. She is a woman that communicates with the Angels. Being in the presence of Doreen changed my life in such an incredible way. My awareness of Angels, healing and life are now so strong that my communications with my Spirit Guide Jooseth and my Guardian Angels are daily. Sometimes it is just a good morning to them, but most of the time I thank them for all that they do for their protection, guidance and love. Being able to see Doreen was a hug from Heaven and the energy received from the hug still lingers and surrounds me whenever I ask for guidance.

Although I communicate with those in the world we cannot see, known as the "other side", and with Angels and Spirit guides and the universe, there are still times when I feel confused, and my self esteem gets low. These are the times when I need a hug, and this is when I knew that you really can get a hug from Heaven if you just sit quiet and ask for one. I was sitting quietly, and I said out loud that I need a hug; I need someone who loves me to hug me. The words had just left my mouth and I felt this wonderful peacefulness surrounding me, and then I felt a wave of warmth and I knew that I was being hugged. It is hard to explain but it was indeed a hug, a hug from Heaven that made me feel so loved, and safe and special. It was a hug that was sent just for me, and a hug I needed. Hugs from Heaven are doses of peacefulness, love and comfort gently covering you like a soft blanket and keeping you safe.

I had just been through one of those days when I felt that I just wanted to retire from working and escape the unpleasant attitude of my manager. During my drive home from work, I started to cry so I turned off the car radio and began to talk to my guardian angels and ask them to help me have harmony in my life. I really dislike my work environment, but I enjoy the job and really needed to have help in turning this negative attitude into a positive one. So I released the situation to them and asked for help and guidance and a sign. I turned the radio back on, and the song now playing was "Faith" this upbeat song by George Michael. I started to laugh at the sign I just received and began to sing along with George Michael "I gotta have faith" soon I was feeling happier and expressed gratitude for the hug from Heaven I just received.

I still have moments of low self esteem, from years of rejection and abuse, but I know that I am not alone and that anytime I need a hug I just have to think of receiving one and the comfort and peace will surround me. Having psychic strength and guidance to help others is very rewarding but also very draining. Sometimes when I am giving a reading the message is also for me and it always surprises me when I hear the words spoken and recognize that the message is both for me and for the person receiving the reading.

Chapter Ten
A Heavenly Hug For You

My life has taken many turns, a divorce, a new partner to share my life with and new career opportunities. I have weathered the storms of abuse, harassment, betrayal and the deaths of my sister Barbie, my brother Terry, and both my parents. I have encountered health problems, weight gain, and financial loss, but I have never lost my faith, my hope and my ability to survive and accept that things happen for a reason. My journey has had many twists in it, and many experiences that served to strengthen my universal connections and psychic abilities. I can now, so easily accept the guidance of my guardian angels, and my spirit guide Jooseth, who walk the journey with me, and guide my steps to keep me safe.

I have comfort in the knowledge that my mother and father played a role in my life on earth to help me better understand the gift of love and the value of trust. If my father hadn't violated his parental role, and if my mother had loved me in the way I so desired, than I would not have understood or appreciated a life that was full of love. Learning through these experiences has taught me to forgive, and move on. I do not have the courage to forget the pain I endured, but I have the wisdom to let it remain in the past, and only call upon it when I need to learn the lesson again, or to share the knowledge with someone else to help them understand how fragile life is and what a wonderful gift it is.

As my journey on earth continues I have no doubt that many more turns will be coming my way as new friends and experiences fill my life. My spiritual journey is the most rewarding, filled with knowledge, wisdom and everlasting peace and love. The powerful communications with the Universe are open to everyone, and everyone receives hugs from Heaven. There are no exceptions, there are plenty of hugs and there is no limit as to how many each one can receive.

Take the time to notice and feel the hugs from Heaven that you receive and make the time for you to give hugs to all in your life that need a hug and to all those you have not met yet. When you give you receive and you will be at peace. Keep love in your heart, keep a smile in your soul, keep tenderness in your speech and gentleness in your touch and you will always feel the hugs from Heaven that are meant for you.

Thank you for taking the time to read my story.

I truly hope that I have opened the door for you to recognize and receive your many hugs from Heaven.

Let this book be one of them!

CPSIA information can be obtained at www.ICGtesting.com
Printed in the USA
LVOW130538220912

299817LV00005B/1/P